Love Lyrics
of Ancient Egypt

o

Acrobatic Dancer. Ostracon. Eighteenth Dynasty. E. Scamuzzi,
Egyptian Art in the Egyptian Museum of Turin (Turin, 1964),
plate LXXIX. Courtesy of the Egyptian Museum of Turin.

Love Lyrics of Ancient Egypt

TRANSLATED BY

BARBARA HUGHES FOWLER

THE UNIVERSITY OF NORTH CAROLINA PRESS

CHAPEL HILL AND

LONDON

o

© 1994 The University of
North Carolina Press.
All rights reserved.
Manufactured in the
United States of America.

The paper in this book meets
the guidelines for permanence
and durability of the Committee
on Production Guidelines
for Book Longevity of the
Council on Library Resources.

Library of Congress
Cataloging-in-Publication Data.

Love lyrics of ancient Egypt /
translated by Barbara Hughes
Fowler.
   p.   cm.
   ISBN 0-8078-2159-4.
— ISBN 0-8078-4468-3 (pbk.)
   1. Egyptian poetry—
Translations into English.
I. Fowler, Barbara Hughes,
1926– .
PJ1945.L67   1994
893'.1—dc20   94-5721
                          CIP

98   97   96   95   94
     5   4   3   2   1

FOR MURRAY FOWLER

IT IS NO secret that I am not an Egyptologist. I have a rudimentary knowledge of hieroglyphics but could not possibly have done these versions of Egyptian lyrics without the scholarly translations, notes, commentary, and transcribed texts of Michael V. Fox's *The Song of Songs and the Ancient Egyptian Love Songs* (Madison, 1985), to which I direct the reader. It was indeed his book that inspired me to translate these enchanting and sweetly erotic poems.

I should like to express my profound gratitude to Richard Jasnow, a true Egyptologist, at the Oriental Institute of the University of Chicago, who read my translations for their fidelity to the letter and tone of the Egyptian and who thereby saved me from several errors, while making other useful observations as well, and to Randall Colaizzi, a poet and classicist at Wellesley College, who read my manuscript for its aesthetic quality and made a number of helpful suggestions. Since I did not in every instance accept their advice, I must emphasize that I alone am responsible for whatever errors or infelicities remain. Finally, I should like to thank Barbara Hanrahan and Ron Maner of the University of North Carolina Press for their gracious help in the preparation of this book.

Singers and Dancers. British Museum, no.37984. Eighteenth Dynasty. Nina M. Davies and A. H. Gardiner, *Ancient Egyptian Paintings* (Chicago and Oxford, 1936), plate LXX. Courtesy of The Oriental Institute of The University of Chicago.

THE POEMS in this volume date to the New Kingdom (ca. 1550–1080 B.C.), a golden age of Egyptian civilization, roughly contemporary with Mycenaean Greece (ca. 1500–1150 B.C.). To the Eighteenth Dynasty (ca. 1550–1305) belong such famous figures as Queen Hatshetsup, who conducted a peaceful reign and built her temple and tomb in the Valley of the Kings opposite Thebes; her son-in-law and husband, the bellicose Thutmose III, who erased her name from her monuments, occupied Palestine and Syria, and campaigned as far as Carcemish on the Euphrates; Akhnaton and his beautiful queen Nefrotete, who fostered an almost monotheistic worship of Aton as a beneficent sun god and inspired a vibrant new naturalism in the visual arts; and Akhnaton's son-in-law, Tutankhamen, whose tomb, with its spectacular treasures, was opened by Howard Carter in 1922. To the Nineteenth Dynasty (ca. 1305–1195) belongs Ramses II, the boastful builder of colossal monuments, and to the Twentieth (ca. 1195–1080) Ramses III, who, like his predecessor, was beset by foreign invaders.

The poems presented here are recorded in the hieratic (cursive) script on documents of the last two of these dynasties, when the glory of the Egyptian Empire was already on the wane. The relevant documents are the Papyrus Harris 500 of the Nineteenth Dynasty, a fragmentary Cairo vase of the Nineteenth or Twentieth Dynasty, the Turin Papyrus of the early Twentieth Dynasty, and the Papyrus Chester Beatty I of the Twentieth Dynasty. The miscellanea are preserved on various fragmentary ostraca and papyri of the Twentieth Dynasty.

We know nothing at all of the immediate setting of the love poems, but the boys and girls who speak them appear to be just that, young persons no more perhaps than thirteen or fourteen years old. "Brother" and "sister" are terms of endearment within the poems and imply no blood relationship. Those who composed these verses were, however, by no means children, for the apparent simplicity of their lines is the result of a highly sophisticated artistry.

The poems may well have been lyrics for songs sung at banquets such as those that can be seen in Egyptian tomb paintings, where women mingle freely with men, although sometimes they are seated on opposite sides of the room. Food is piled sumptuously on tables, and servants move about offering food, wine, and fresh cones of the perfumed ointment that the women wear upon their heads. Musicians, who during the New Kingdom were women more often than men, play harps, lyres, lutes, clarinets, and oboes while others sing or dance, acrobatically or more sedately, to their tunes. The women guests wear gowns of pleated white linen, are adorned with elaborate wigs, and are beautifully made-up. The paint applied around the eyes, which the girls of the poems mention, was either green or black, though the black kohl was more popular than the malachite green during the New Kingdom. Among artifacts surviving from antiquity are samples of wigs, linen garments, and many cosmetic boxes and tools such as those depicted or suggested in the tomb paintings and in the lyrics translated here.

The love lyrics reflect the tomb paintings in other ways as well: in their allusions to fishing and fowling, to plants and trees, and above all to color—jasper red, malachite and feldspar green, lapis lazuli blue. The tomb painters had as basic colors on their palettes white (chalk or gypsum), black (carbon), red (iron oxides), blue (a compound of silica, copper, and calcium), green (powdered malachite, a natural copper ore), yellow (yellow ochre or, during the New Kingdom, orpiment, a naturally occurring sulfide of arsenic). By mixing these the artists were able to produce many secondary colors, for instance, gray, pink, and brown.[1]

The poems of this collection should, in their innocent sensuousness, give the lie to the popular conception of the Egyptians as a gloomy people, obsessed with death. Nothing could be further from the truth. From the very beginnings of their identity as a people, their hieroglyphs—which abound

---

1. T. G. H. James, *Egyptian Painting and Drawing in the British Museum* (Cambridge, Mass., 1986), 11–12.

in signs of animals (bulls, calves, horses, asses, kids, newborn hartebeests, rams, pigs, cats, hounds, jackals, lions, panthers, hippopotami, elephants, giraffes, oryxes, gazelles, ibexes, baboons, monkeys, desert hares), plants (especially the lotus and the papyrus), and birds (vultures, buzzards, falcons, owls, guinea fowls, hoopoes, lapwings, ibises, flamingos, jabirus, herons, egrets, pintail ducks, quail chicks, plovers)— attest to their delight in the fecundity of the Nile Valley. These signs were, to be sure, originally emblems for the creatures themselves, but their retention as phonemes and determinatives, exquisitely carved and painted, reveals the Egyptians' joy in the flora and fauna of this present world. So, on a larger scale, do the paradisiacal tomb paintings, with their gorgeously colored panoramas of life on this earth, declare that the elaborate preparations for death of those who could afford to make them were but another aspect of their passionate desire to go on living. Egyptian nobles and kings fully intended to hunt, fish, fowl, eat, drink, and get drunk at banquets throughout eternity.

I am translating documents that are replete with lacunae, scribal corruption, unidentified words (especially the names of plants), and word play, which even if it were not so obscure to us as it often is, would probably be impossible to render adequately in English. Often I am translating restorations of the text that may well be wide of the mark. Sometimes too I have for the sake of the meter or simply to close a lacuna supplied a word of my own. In three places (20E, 21F, and 35) I have translated a word that means "lady" or "mistress" as "sister," in order to avoid the Elizabethan flavor of the former. Rather than disfigure my text with brackets, I have confessed to the more significant of these sins in my notes. On the whole, however, I have been as faithful to the original texts as I reasonably could while still making English poems out of these Egyptian songs. I have followed Fox[2] in my numbering of the poems.

---

2. Michael V. Fox, *The Song of Songs and the Ancient Egyptian Love Songs* (Madison, 1985).

Nubian Women and Children. Tomb of Haremhab (no. 78). Eighteenth Dynasty. Nina M. Davies and A. H. Gardiner, *Ancient Egyptian Paintings* (Chicago and Oxford, 1936), plate xxxix. Courtesy of The Oriental Institute of The University of Chicago.

Papyrus Harris

500

o

GROUP A

Girl) AM I NOT here with you?
     Where do you direct
your heart? Ought you not
     to embrace me? Has
my act come back . . . ?
     . . . the amusement . . .
if you attempt to caress
     my thighs . . .

Is it because you've thought
     of food that you'd go forth?
Is it because you've become
     a man of your belly you'd go?
Is it because you care
     about clothes that you'd go?
I have a linen sheet.
     Is it because you're hungry
you'd go? Then take
     hold of my breasts that their milk
flow forth for you. Better
     a day in my brother's embrace
than ten-thousand thousands

          . . . .

Girl)   YOUR LOVE is mixed in my limbs
            like honey mixed with water,
      like mandragoras
            mixed with resin gum,
      or the blending of flour with salt.
            Hurry to see your sister,
      like a steed to the battlefield,
            like a . . .
      . . . its plants . . .
            while heaven grants to you,
      like a soldier's arrival, my love.[3]

---

3. In this and other poems "mandragora," an aphrodisiac, is a conjectural rendering of *rrmt*, a fruit of erotic significance. Some of the other ingredients mentioned here appear in medical texts. I have supplied the word "salt."

Boy)   THE MARSH'S plants bewilder.
        My sister's mouth is a lotus,
    her breasts mandragoras,
        her arms the limbs of a tree,
    her . . .
        her head the love-wood trap,
    and I am the gone goose!
        The cord is my . . .
    her hair is the lure in the net
        that will ensnare me.[4]

---

4. "Mouth" is not preserved in the original. "Limbs
of a tree" is also conjecture.

Girl) MY HEART'S not lenient yet
      to your making of love,
my little jackal cub!
      Your beer is your making of love.
I will not abandon it
      until I'm banished by blows
to spend my days in the marsh
      or blows banish me
to Syria with sticks and rods,
      to Nubian land with palms,
to the highlands with willow whips,
      to the lowlands with cudgeling.
I will not heed their advice
      to abandon the boy I love.

Boy)　I'M SAILING north with the stream
　　　　to the captain's stroke of the oars,
　　　my bundle of reeds on my back.
　　　　I'm going toward Ankh-Towy,
　　　where I shall say to Ptah,
　　　　the Lord God of Truth,
　"Give me my sister tonight."

　　The river is like wine,
　　　　its reeds the god Ptah,
　　Sekhmet its lotus buds,
　　　　Yadit its lotus buds,
　　Nefertem its lotus buds.
　　　　The earth has grown light
　　through my sister's loveliness.
　　　　Memphis is a bowl
　　of mandragoras set before
　　　　Ptah, the Gracious One.[5]

---

5. Ankh-Towy is the necropolis of Memphis, an
important cult center of the god Ptah, the shaper
of the world and father of gods and men. Lord of
Truth is his epithet as judge of the dead. Sekhmet
is the goddess of disease and war. Nefertem is the
son of Sekhmet and Ptah. Yadit (I3dt = Dew?)
is an otherwise unknown goddess. The Gracious
One is Ptah.

Boy) I WILL lie down within
       and feign to be ill, and then
my neighbors will come to see.
       My sister will enter with them.
She'll put the physicians to shame,
       for she will understand
that I am sick for love.

Boy) THIS IS my sister's mansion.
          At the center is her entrance.
     Her double doors are ajar,
          her latch is drawn back.
     My sister is incensed.
          Were I the keeper of
     her door, I'd enkindle her
          and hear her voice enraged,
     like a child afraid of her.

Girl) I'M SAILING to the north
             along the Ruler's Canal.
          I've entered Pre's Canal.
             My heart's intent to see
          the preparation of booths
             at the gate of the Ity Canal.

          I shall hasten with never a pause
             since my heart has thought of Pre.
          Then I shall see my brother
             enter. He's going toward
          the Houses of . . .

             I stand beside you at
          the gate of the Ity Canal,
             for you have brought my heart
          to Heliopolis.

             Now I've withdrawn with you
          to the trees of the Houses of . . .
             . . . .
          to gather the leaves of the Houses
             of . . .
          to make them a fan for me.
             I shall see what it does!

I'm going to the Garden
    of Love. My bosom is filled
with persea fruit, my hair
    is drenched with balm. I am
a noblewoman. I am
    Queen of the Two Lands,
whenever I am with you.[6]

---

6. Pre is the sun god. The Canal of Pre is the eastern
branch of the Nile, which waters the area of Heliopolis. The Ity Canal joined Heliopolis with the Nile.
Persea fruit is associated with fertility; it matures in
the season of the Nile's rising. The Two Lands are
Upper and Lower Egypt. "Whenever I am with
you" is restored.

Fishing and Fowling in the Marshes. Thebes, tomb of Menna (no.69). Eighteenth Dynasty. Nina M. Davies and A. H. Gardiner,

Papyrus Harris

500

○

GROUP B

Girl)   HOW LOVELY is your sister,
      the darling of your heart,
as she comes dancing back
      from the fresh meadow grass!

My brother, my beloved,
      my heart craves your love,
all that you created,
      and so to you I say,
look at all that happened:
      I came to trap birds.
I had in my one hand
      a snare, in the other a cage,
and also my woven mat.
      All the birds of Punt[7]
have alighted on Egypt,
      and all are anointed with myrrh.
The first takes my bait.
      His fragrance comes from Punt.
His claws are caught with balm.
      My heart longs for you.
Let us both release
      the bait. I was alone,
rejoicing in you. I let
      you hear my alluring call

---

7. Punt is an area of the eastern Sudan, bordering
on Ethiopia. It was famous for its spices and became
for the Egyptians a half-legendary land.

for the lovely bird anointed
    with myrrh. You are here,
and so I set the snare.
    Going to the meadow
is pleasant indeed for him
    who loves to do it.

Girl) THE VOICE of the goose sounds forth
  as he's caught by the bait. Your love
ensnares me. I can't let it go.
  I shall take home my nets,
but what shall I tell my mother,
  to whom I return every day
laden with lovely birds?
  I set no traps today,
ensnared as I was by love.

Girl)   THE SOARING goose alights,
            while lesser birds still fly,
      and flutters all my garden.
            Only you, my love, excite me.
      My heart balances
            with yours. From your beauty
      may I never be apart.

Girl)   I HAVE abandoned my brother.
      When I remember your love,
my heart within stands still.
      When I see sweet cakes,
they taste to me like salt.
      Pomegranate wine
was sweet once in my mouth.
      Now it is the gall
of birds. The scent of your nose
      alone restores my heart.
I have forevermore
      Amon's gift to me.[8]

---

8. The beginning of this poem is lost. "Scent of your
nose" refers to the practice of "nose-kissing": the
couple rubbed noses and smelled one another's
faces to express their affection. Amon is the god of
Thebes. "When I remember your love" is literally
"to go forth [. . .] of / in your love."

Girls Bringing Fruit and Flowers. Thebes, tomb of Menna (no.69).
Eighteenth Dynasty. Nina M. Davies and A. H. Gardiner, *Ancient
Egyptian Paintings* (Chicago and Oxford, 1936), plate LII.
Courtesy of The Oriental Institute of The University of Chicago.

Girl)   THE LOVELIEST thing has happened!
  My heart hopes to be
the mistress of your house,
  while your arm rests on my breast,
for my love encompasses you.
  I pray to my heart within,
"Give me my prince tonight,
  or I shall be like a girl
who lies, dead, in her grave!"
  For are you not health and life?
The very sight of your face
  will make me rejoice for your health,
for my heart is seeking for you.[9]

---

9. "My heart hopes to be the mistress of your house"
is much restored. "Give me" in "Give me my prince
tonight" is also based on a restoration.

Girl)   THE VOICE of the dove speaks
              "The day has already dawned.
         When will you go home?"
              Be quiet, bird. Don't scold.
         I found my brother in
              the chamber of his bed
         and exceedingly my heart
              rejoiced. We speak together:
         "I'll never be apart.
              Our hands will be entwined
         as I stroll about with you
              in every pleasant place."
         He sees me as the best
              of the most beautiful.
         He has not wounded my heart.

Girl)   I TURN my face to the door.
       My brother comes to me.
    I turn my eyes to the road.
          I listen for the crack
    of the neglectful one's whip.
          I consider my brother's love
    my solitary concern.
          Because of my love for him
    my heart cannot be silent.
          It sends a messenger
    to me, fleet of foot,
          whether to or fro,
    to tell me how my brother
          has done me wrong. In short:
    he's found another who gazes
          at his face. Well,
    what do I care that another
          with cruel and cunning heart
    makes me a stranger now?

Girl)   I THOUGHT of my love for you
while only half my hair
was put up. I've come
in haste to find you
with my hair hanging down,
although my dress and locks
have been ready all along.

Girl)   Portulaca¹¹

MY HEART has a portion of yours.
I do its will for you
when I am in your arms.
My prayer is the paint of my eyes.
The sight of you makes bright
my eyes. I come close
to see your love for me.
Beloved lord of my heart!
How lovely my hour with you!
It flows forever for me
since first I lay with you.
Whether in sorrow or joy,
you have exalted my heart.
Never leave me, I beg.

---

10. Each of the three poems (17, 18, 19) comprising
"The Flower Song" begins with the name of a
flower or tree. The following line then makes a
word-play upon this name.

11. mḫmḫ in the opening line is, scholars conjecture,
the portulaca.

Girl)   IN IT ARE *s'3m* [12] trees.
            One is exalted there.
        Your favorite sister am I
            like a field of fragrant blooms,
        an abundance of blossoming buds.
            Lovely the channel within
        which your hand dug out while we
            cooled in the north wind.
        A lovely place for a stroll
            while you hold your hand in mine.
        My body luxuriates,
            my heart exults as we walk
        together. The sound of your voice
            is pomegranate wine.
        I draw nourishment
            from hearing it. Could I
        with each and every glance
            behold you, it would be better
        for me than food or drink.

---

12. *s'3m* cannot be identified.

Girl)   IN IT ARE $\underline{t}\mathfrak{z}yt$ [13] flowers.
　　　I took your wreaths away
　　when you came home drunk and fell
　　　　asleep in your bed. I chafed
　　your feet while children . . .

　　　　　. . . . .
　　At dawn I delight. May life
　　　　and health be ever yours!

---

13. $\underline{t}\mathfrak{z}yt$ is unidentified.

Detail of *Fishing and Fowling in the Marshes*. Thebes, tomb of Menna (no.69). Eighteenth Dynasty. Nina M. Davies and A. H. Gardiner, *Ancient Egyptian Paintings* (Chicago and Oxford, 1936), plate LV. Courtesy of The Oriental Institute of The University of Chicago.

Cairo
Love Songs

o

Girl)   I DWELL upon your love
      through the night and all
the day, through the hours
     I lie asleep and when
I wake again at dawn.
. . . .
Your beauty nourishes hearts.
     Your voice creates desire.
It makes my body strong.
     " . . . he is weary . . ."
So may I say whenever . . .
     There is no other girl
in harmony with his heart.
     I am the only one.[14]

---

14. "I dwell upon" is based upon a restoration.
"Your voice creates desire" is my guess; the text is
"Desire . . . your voice."

Girl)　YOUR LOVE is as longed for
　　　　　as honey mixed with oil
　　on the limbs of noblemen,
　　　　　as linen on bodies of gods,
　　as incense to the nose.
　　　　. . . . . . .
　　It's like a mandragora
　　　　　held in a man's hand.
　　It's like the dates a man
　　　　　mixes into his beer.
　　It's like the salt a man
　　　　　adds to his daily bread.
　　. . . . .
　　We will be together
　　　　　even in the days
　　of the peace of old age.
　　　　　I will be with you
　　every day to set
　　　　　before you food as though
　　I were a serving maid
　　　　　attendant upon her master.

Girl)   MY GOD, my lotus, my love,
      the north wind is blowing.
How pleasant to reach the river!
    . . . breath . . .
      . . . flower . . .
My heart longs to go down
    to bathe before you
to show you my loveliness
    in a tunic of expensive
royal linen, drenched
    in *tišps* oil, my hair
braided in plaits like reeds.
    I'll enter the river with you
and come out carrying
    a red fish for you
splendid in my fingers.
    I'll offer it to you
as I behold your beauty.
    O my hero, my brother, my love,
come and behold me.[15]

---

15. *tišps* is unidentified.

Boy)   MY BELOVED sister
                 is on the other bank.
         The river washes my limbs.
             The waters of the flood
         are ferocious in their season.
             A crocodile awaits
         upon the sandbank.
                 Yet I have gone down
         to the waters of the Nile
                 that I may wade the flood,
         my heart brave in its rush.
                 The crocodile was a mouse,
         the flood dry land to my feet.
                 It is my sister's love
         that makes me strong. She casts
                 a water spell for me.
         I behold my heart's beloved.
                 She stands before my face.

Boy)   MY SISTER has come to me.
          My heart is filled with joy.
     I open my arms wide
          that I may embrace her.
     My heart is as happy in
          my breast as a red fish
     swimming in its pond.
          O night, you are mine
     forever, since my sister
          has come in love to me.

Boy) I SHALL embrace her.
Her arms are opened wide.
I'm like a man from Punt.
It's like the *misy* plant
which becomes a medicine.
Her fragrance is *ibr* balm.[16]

----

16. *misy* and *ibr* are unidentified.

Boy)   I SHALL kiss my sister.
           She parts her lips for me.
     I am delirious
           even without beer.
     How the lack has been
           fulfilled. The goddess Menqet[17]
     is decorated there.
           She conducts me to
     my sister's bed. Come,
           that I may speak to you.
     Put fine linen about
           her limbs and spread
     her bed with royal cloth.
           Attend to the white linens
     of adornment. Her limbs
           are as lovely as anything drenched
     in oil from the *tišps* tree.

     ———————————

     17. Menqet is the goddess of beer.

A Lady Guest and Serving-Maids. Thebes, tomb of Djeserkaraʻsonb (no. 38). Eighteenth Dynasty. Nina M. Davies and A. H. Gardiner, *Ancient Egyptian Paintings* (Chicago and Oxford, 1936), plate xxxvi. Courtesy of The Oriental Institute of The University of Chicago.

Boy) WOULD that I were
her Nubian slave,
her servant in secret!

She brings to my beloved
mandragoras in a bowl
which she holds in her hand
as she gratifies my lust.

She'd allow me then the color
of all her naked body.

Boy) WOULD that I were,
if only for a month,
the launderer of
my sister's linen cloth!

I'd gather strength
from just the grasp
of the clothes that touch
my beloved's body.

For it would be I
who'd wash from her scarf
the moringa oils.
I'd rub then my body
with the clothes
that she'd cast off
and she'd . . .

What bliss I'd have,
what utter delight!

How vigorous would
my body be!

Boy) WOULD that I were
her delicate signet ring,
her finger's sentinel!
I'd see then her love
each and every day
. . . .
And it would be I
who'd stolen her heart.

Boy)   WOULD that I had
a morning of looking,
like the bronze that spends
a lifetime with her!
Lovely the land of Isy
and precious its tribute!
Joyous the mirror
receiving her gaze![18]

18. The tribute of Isy (which may have been the
island of Cyprus) included copper. The boy is
singing about the bronze mirror into which the
girl is gazing.

Boy) WOULD that my sister were mine
each and every day,
like the freshness of green
that a wreath weaves in!
The river reeds are dried.
The safflower has blossomed.
The lotuses are clustered.
The mandragoras
and lapis lazuli shoots
have sprouted forth.

The buds from Hatti are ripe.
The myristica has bloomed.
The willow has greened.
She would be with me
each and every day
like the freshness of green
that a wreath weaves in.

. . . .

All the meadow blossoms
with burgeoning buds.[19]

---

19. Hatti is the land of the Hittites. In the line
"The lotuses have clustered," I have, for reasons
of euphony entirely, written "lotuses" for *mrbb*
flowers, which are unidentified, but which are
almost certainly not lotuses.

Boy) WOULD that she might come
that I could behold her!
I'd keep festival to the god
who'd hold her not apart again.
May he grant me my sister every day.
May she never be distant from me.
If for a moment I am apart from her,
my stomach is aflutter.
I hasten to respond.

Boy) WOULD that[20] . . .
        . . . his soul.
        I shall honor that god
        with loveliness of the night
        and keep a feast for him.
        May my heart descend to its place.
        . . . it
        . . . every suffering from my limbs
            . . . who seeks the sister
        whose body I dare not approach.
        She'll banish my lovesick ills.

---

20. "Would that" is restored in this poem.

Song of the Sycamore. Papyrus. Eighteenth Dynasty. E. Scamuzzi, *Egyptian Art in the Egyptian Museum of Turin* (Turin, 1964), plate LXXIX. Courtesy of the Egyptian Museum of Turin.

*Turin
Love Song*

o

THE PERSEA tree moves
    his mouth and speaks to me:
"My pits are like her teeth.
    My fruit is like her breasts.
I am the best of the trees
    in the orchard. I stand steadfast
in all the seasons that
    the sister spends with her brother.
They sit in my spreading shade
    while drunk with the wine of grape
and pomegranate, while bathed
    in balm and moringa oil.
All the trees except
    for me have shed their leaves
in the meadow. Only I
    flower all year in the garden.
I've lasted. I've cast a blossom
    but have next year's bloom
already within me.
    Of all the trees I am
the best and yet I'm seen
    as second best. If this
occurs again, I'll not
    be silent for them . . .
. . . for her friend.
    Then shall the sin be seen,

the sister disciplined.
　　She won't spend the day again
with their lotuses and staves,
　　with blossoms and lotus buds,
with unguents of fine oils
　　and balms of every kind.
May she instead make you
　　spend in merriment
the day in a hut of reeds
　　set in a secret place.
Truly he goes forth.
　　Let us flatter him.
Force him to spend the day
　　in his shelter together with us." [21]

———

21. A fair amount of this text is restored.

THE SYCAMORE-fig moves
    his foliage [22] mouth and speaks:
"Consider what I will do.
    I'll come to the girl. Is there
any tree as noble as I?
    And yet, if there are no slaves,
I'll be the Syrian slave,
    booty brought for his
beloved girl. She had
    me planted in her orchard
but poured no libation for me
    upon the day of drinking.
She did not fill my belly
    with water from the skins.
I was just for her amusement,
    abandoned without a drink.
As my soul lives, I swear,
    O my beloved girl,
this will come back to you!"

------

22. The word "foliage" does not occur in the
Egyptian text. I added it for the sake of the meter.

THE LITTLE sycamore
　　that the girl planted with
her own hands opens
　　her foliage mouth and speaks.
The drops of sap in her mouth
　　are like the honey of bees.
She is a beauty, her leaves
　　lovely, flourishing
and verdant, laden with fruit,
　　both ripe and green. She is
redder than red jasper.
　　Her leaves are malachite.
Her bark is faience ware.
　　Her wood is feldspar green,
her berries like the myristica's.
　　She draws those not beneath.
Her shadow cools the air.
　　She puts a note into
the hand of a little girl,
　　her chief gardener's child,
and sends her speeding to
　　the beloved sister to say:
"Come and pass the time
　　where the young are gathering.
The meadow celebrates
　　its day. Beneath me
are a festival booth and a hut.
　　My gardeners rejoice
at the sight of you." Send
　　your servants ahead of you,

carrying their cups.
    One becomes drunk just
hastening to me,
    without a single sip.
Your attendants have come.
    They've brought all their supplies:
beer of every sort
    and bread of every kind,
vegetables in plenty,
    today's and yesterday's,
and every delicious fruit.
    Spend the day in delight,
a morning and another,
    reclining in my shade.
"Her brother is at her right.
    She gets him drunk and does
whatever he desires.
    The festival's beer hut
is disarranged from drink,
    but she is still with her brother.
The linen clothes are spread
    beneath me, while she,
the sister, is strolling about,
    but I am secret of belly.
I will not say that I
    have seen their spoken words." [23]

---

23. In this, as in the preceding, poem I have supplied
"foliage" for the sake of meter.

Toilet of a Beauty. Papyrus. Twentieth Dynasty. E. Scamuzzi, *Egyptian Art in the Egyptian Museum of Turin* (Turin, 1964), plate LXXIX. Courtesy of the Egyptian Museum of Turin.

Papyrus
Chester Beatty
I

Boy)   MY SISTER is one alone.
            Most gracious of all women,
    she has among them no peer.
        Behold, she is like Sothis
    when she rises to herald the flood
            of the Nile and fertility
    for the year.[24] Precious, aglow,
            with incandescent skin,
    her eyes dazzle with gazing.
        Sweet her lips as she speaks,
    She spends no excess of words.
        Her neck is like a swan's,
    her breast is whiter than sand.
        Her hair is lapis lazuli,
    her arms more precious than gold,
            her fingers like lotuses.
    Rounded her buttocks but bound
            her waist. Her thighs complete
    her loveliness. Enchanting
            her walk as she strolls upon
    the land. She captures my heart
            in her embrace. She turns

---

24. Sothis is Sirius, the Dog Star. It rose at the time
of the flooding of the Nile and so was associated
with the fertility of the land. The Egyptian here is
simply "She is like Sothis arisen at the beginning
of the good year," but I have expanded the text to
explain why the year was "good."

the heads of all the men
    who behold her. Bliss
is his who can embrace her.
    Of lovers he's foremost.
Her coming forth is like
    the rising of Sothis the star.

Girl) MY BROTHER'S voice disturbs
    my heart and makes me ill.
Although he is among
    the neighbors of my mother,
I cannot go to him.
    My mother is very good
at commanding me and says,
    "Do not visit him."
Nevertheless, my heart
    is vexed when I think of him,
for my love has captured me.
    He is confused of heart,
and I am just the same!
    He does not know how I
long to embrace him
    or he would send a message
to my mother. O my brother,
    I am decreed for you
by Hathor, the Golden One.[25]
    Come to me that I
may behold your loveliness,
    and may my father and mother
rejoice. May all the people
    rejoice in you together,
rejoice, my brother, in you!

---

25. The Golden One, Hathor, is the goddess of love.

Boy) MY HEART intended to see
      her loveliness while I sat
within her house. I found
      Mehi on my way.
He rode upon a chariot
      together with his lovers.
I cannot possess myself
      before him. I ought to go
easily past him.
      But see, the Nile is a road,
and I know not the place
      of my feet. Foolish my heart
indeed! Why stride
      easily past Mehi?
If I pass him by,
      I'll tell him of my turnings:
"I belong to you,"
      I'll say, and he will flaunt
my name and attach me to
      the primary band of ensnared
who are companions of him.[26]

26. Mehi is a mysterious figure of whom Fox ten-
tatively says, "He is a Cupid-figure who embodies
the power of love. He wanders about the earth and
holds young people captive in the bonds of love.
Whoever turns himself over to love becomes one of
Mehi's followers, one of the *kpwy* ('trapped ones'?),
who are apparently none other than the group of
males called 'the lovers' " (p. 66).

Girl)   MY HEART quickly flits
            away when I remember
your love. It does not let
            me go as humans go
but has leapt from its proper place.
            It does not allow me to don
a tunic. I cannot put on
            my cloak. I cannot paint
my eyes. I cannot anoint
            with balm my body at all.
"Don't give up until
            you've got inside his house!"
So speaks my heart to me
            when I remember him.
Do not, my heart, create
            folly in me. Why
do you behave so
            crazily? Be still.
Be cool until your brother
            comes to you. Then I
shall do just such things.
            Don't let people say,
"This girl collapsed because
            she was so much in love."
Be staunch, my heart, whenever
            you think of him. Do not
like an animal scurry away.

Boy)   I SHALL praise the Golden One,
   exalt her majesty,
extol the Mistress of Heaven,
   give homage to the goddess
Hathor, thanks to my Lady.
   I shall call upon her
to hear my supplication
   and destine my sister for me.
Of her own wish she came
   to me. How wonderful was
what happened to me! I became
   joyous and happy and strong
when I said, "Ah, here she is!"
   No sooner had she come
than the lovers bowed down
   because of the might of her love.
And so I'll pray to Hathor
   to grant me my sister as
a gift. Three whole days
   have gone by since I
made supplication for her,
   but for these five full days
has she been gone from me.

Girl)   I PASSED close to his house
             and discovered his door ajar.
       My brother stood beside
             his mother and all his kin.
       Love for him ensnares
             the heart of everyone
       who strolls along the road.
             A precious boy! He has
       no peer. His character's
             beyond reproach. My brother
       gazed at me as I
             walked by, but I exult alone.
       How happily my heart
             rejoices, O my brother,
       since first I beheld you!
             If my mother knew
       my heart, she'd go inside
             his house for a little while.
       O Golden One,
             put that thought in her head.
       Then I'd hasten to
             my brother and kiss him before
       his companions, nor would I be
             embarrassed before them all.
       I'd rejoice to have them see
             that you are acquainted with me.
       I'd keep festival to
             my goddess. My heart leaps
       to go forth and gaze upon
             my beloved brother tonight.
       How lovely the passing by!

63

Boy)   IT'S SEVEN whole days since I
have seen my sister. A sickness
pervades me. My limbs are lead.
I barely sense my body.
Should physicians come,
their drugs could not cure
my heart, nor could the priests
diagnose my disease.
Should they say, "Here
she is," that would heal me.
Her name would restore me.
Should her messengers
come and go, that
is what would revive my heart.
More potent than medicine
my sister is to me.
More powerful too is she
than the Compendium.[27]
Her arrival from outside
is my amulet. At the sight
of her I regain my health.
She widens her eyes at me,
and my body becomes young.
She speaks and I am strong.
I embrace her. She banishes
the sickness from me. But she
has left me for seven whole days.

----

27. The Compendium is a medical text.

Girl) WOULD that you'd come to your sister
            as swiftly as a king's
        messenger whose master's
            heart longs to hear
        the news. His stable's steeds
            are harnessed for him, and he
        has horses standing in wait
            at all the resting posts.
        His chariot is accoutered.
            No respite for him on the road.
        Only when he has arrived
            at his sister's house will his heart
        have reason to rejoice.

Girl) WOULD that you'd come to your sister
    as swiftly as a steed
belonging to the king,
    the choicest of a thousand,
the stables' very prince.
    As is his provender,
so also is his pace.
    His master knows his gait.
If he hears the crack of the whip,
    he cannot be constrained.
No chieftain of foreign hordes
    can overtake him in speed.
How the heart of his sister knows
    that he's not far away!

Girl)   WOULD that you'd come to your sister
     as swiftly as a gazelle
that bounds across the sands.
     Its legs are atremble, its body
exhausted, for fear pervades
     its limbs. A hunter with hound
pursues him, but they can't see
     even his dust. He regards
a resting place as a snare.
     The river he takes as a road.
Before you can kiss your hand
     four times, you'll have arrived
at her cave. You'll pursue
     your sister's love, for Hathor,
the Golden One, it is
     who destines her for you.

Poet)   WHEN YOU bring it to
               your sister's house and storm
           her cave, her gate will be raised
               that the keeper of the house
           may slaughter it. And supply
               her with song and acrobatic
           dance, with ale and wine
               for her to set aside
           that you may intoxicate her
               and fulfill her lust in a night.[29]
           And then she'll say to you,
               "Take me in your embrace,
           and when the dawn breaks,
               that's how we'll be found."

---

28. Nakhtsobek is the name of the scribe.

29. "That you may intoxicate her and fulfill her
lust in a night" is my translation of a very obscure
passage. The Egyptian seems to mean something
like "that you may make confused / disordered her
[possessive adjective] . . . you make complete / finish
her/it in her night."

Poet) WHEN YOU bring it to
     your sister's hall,
while you are all alone,
     you may satisfy
your lust in her love's snare.
     A winnowing wind will blow
lightly through the house
     and the heavens descend in a breeze.
They will not blow away
     her fragrance but bring it to you,
an intoxicating aroma
     encompassing those who are there.
The Golden One sends her
     as a gift to you that you
may complete the days of your life.

Boy)   HOW SKILLFULLY my sister
          casts the lasso, and yet
     she ropes no cattle in.
          With her hair she ensnares me.
     With her eyes she fetters me.
          With her thighs she binds me fast.
     With her seal she burns the brand.

Girl)　WHILE YOU argued with your heart —
　　　　"Take her in your embrace" —
　　　by Amon, I came to you,
　　　　　my dress still disarranged.[30]

---

30. "My dress still disarranged" is literally "my tunic
on my shoulder."

Girl) MY BROTHER is standing at
the watercourse. He plants
his foot on the river bank.
He prepares an altar to spend
the festive day with beers
of the choicest kinds. He grants
me the hue of his naked loins.
Longer it is than wide.

Boy)   FOR WHAT my sister did—
            shall I be silent to her?
        She left me standing at
            her house's door. She went
        inside and did not say
            "A pleasant welcome home,"
        but to the night I'd spend
            with her she blocked her ears.

Boy) I PASSED her house befogged.
        I knocked. It was not opened
to me. A wonderful night
        for our keeper of the door!
Bolt, I'll open you!
        Door, you are my death,
an evil spirit for me.
        We'll slaughter an ox inside.
O door, do not expend
        your wrath that sacrifice
of oxen be made to your bolt,
        fatlings to your threshold,
a plump goose to your posts,
        to your lintel an oriole.
Every succulent piece
        of our ox we will save
for Ptah, the carpenter lad,
        that he may make us a bolt
of reeds, a door of palm.

Then the brother can come
and discover an open house,[31]
a bed, spread with linen
of delicate weave, and a pretty
little maidservant too,
who will say to me
". . . the mayor."

---

31. "Then the brother can come and discover an
open house" is literally "then the brother can come
at any time."

Bull Decked Out for Sacrifice, Thebes, tomb of an unknown noble (no.226). Eighteenth Dynasty. Nina M. Davies and

Miscellanea

o

Girl)　IF THE wind comes, it blows
toward the sycamore tree.
If you come, you blow
on the wind toward me.[32]

---

32. "You blow on the wind toward me" is
completely restored.

Girl)   HE IS THE love-wolf
gobbling in my cave,
within . . . the pebbles beneath
. . .the moringa tree
. . . eating of the bread
offered to the gods.

Girl) TURN ME over. Attend
to your limbs. Direct
your face to the wall and you'll
deprive your longing heart
of the body's satisfaction.

Boy)　I PASS the day imploring
　　　　my beloved sister,
　　　　"Don't do that to me, my lady.
　　　　Don't keep me waiting like this."
　　　　I'll take my mare before
　　　　the wind because of her love.
　　　　I'll lay me down beside
　　　　the waters of . . .
　　　　the message . . .

Boy)   THE LADY sails to the north,
drinking beer . . .
An island lies before him
. . . sail
cool . . .
. . . gold unalloyed.
Drunkenly we'll dance.

We'll place our gifts before
Mehi the King and say,
"Spend the day with love!" 33

---

33. "Spend the day with love" is my invention.
The text is "love. Spend the day."

Boy [?]) HOW SWEET is the brewed beer
 when I am at his side
 and my hands are touching him!
 The breezes blow as I say
 in my heart, "Let's get drunk
 on this sweet wine, for I
 am consecrated to you[34]
 through the powers . . ."

---

34. "I am consecrated to you" is literally "I am upon
your spirit (*ka*)."

Boy)   MY BELOVED sister's body [35]

. . . .

Her necklace is made of buds.
Her bones are delicate reeds.
She wears a signet ring
and has a lotus in
her hand. I kiss her before
everyone that they
all may see my love.
She enraptures my heart, and when
she sees me, I am refreshed.

----

35. *mr* at the beginning of the poem may be a verb,
i.e., "my sister loves in/through the body" or "the
love of my sister [is] in the . . . [of] body."